I0143121

SEED OF DARKNESS
The Final Tale of Edgar Allan Poe

A Play in Two Acts
by
Lawrence Riggins

Peregrine Capital Publishers

Virginia Poe

For Shirley, with love and apologies...

There is a land of the living and a land of the dead and the bridge
is love, the only survival, the only meaning.
-- Thornton Wilder

Easy is the descent to the Lower World; but, to retrace your steps
and to escape to the upper air -- this is the task, this the toil.
-- The Aeneid

Copyright © 2011/1987 by Lawrence Riggins.

All rights reserved. No part of this book may be reproduced in any form or by any electronic or mechanical means, or the facilitation thereof, including information storage and retrieval systems without permission in writing from the publisher, except by a reviewer, who may quote brief passages in a review. Any members of educational institutions wishing to photocopy part or all of the work for classroom use, or publishers who would like to obtain permission to include the work in an anthology, should send their inquiries to www.peregrinecapitalpublishers.com.

CAUTION: Professionals and amateurs are hereby warned that Seed of Darkness, The Final Tale of Edgar Allan Poe is subject to royalties. They are fully protected under the copyright laws of the United States, Canada, United Kingdom, and all British Commonwealth countries, and all countries covered by the International Copyright Union, the Pan American Copyright Convention, and the Universal Copyright Convention. All rights including professional, amateur, motion picture, recitation, public reading, radio broadcasting, television, video or sound taping, all other forms of mechanical or electronic reproduction, such as information storage and retrieval systems and photocopying, and rights of translation into foreign languages, are strictly reserved.

First-class professional, stock, and amateur applications for permission to perform -- and those other rights stated above -- must be made in advance before rehearsals begin to www.peregrinecapitalpublishers.com or www.hollywoodstructure.com.

Printed in the United States of America

Riggins, Lawrence, 1959-

Seed of Darkness, The Final Tale of Edgar Allan Poe / Lawrence Riggins

1.Poe, Edgar Allan, 1809-1849-Drama. 2. Poets-American-Drama. 3. Detective-Drama

ISBN-978-0-9832222-0-0

Design by Dan Asahi
Interior illustration: Virginia Poe. First portrait by Thomas Sully.

Peregrine Capital Publishers
www.peregrinecapitalpublishers.com

Hollywood Structure Books
www.hollywoodstructure.com

CONTENTS

SEED OF DARKNESS was first produced at Northern Kentucky University with the following cast:

EDGAR POE	Nick Dantos
ELMIRA	Deana Rae Elliott
VIRGINIA	Mia Renee
WHITMAN	Karen Lynn Burton
MARY/LADY #2	Patricia A. Blessing
MRS. ELIOT	Patricia LaRosa
GRISWOLD	D. Troy Hitch
BRIGGS/ROYSTER	Ty Harwell
INSPECTOR	Joseph Garret Sturgeon
DANNY	Illya Haase
MRS. CLEMM/LADY #1	Linette Katherine Comley
SHELTON	David Rosenberg
DEPUTY	Peter B. Sears
LAURIE/BLATHERSKITE #1	Christina Maria Wright
BETH/BLATHERSKITE #2	Caroline Elizabeth Asher

Director	Ken Jones
Stage Manager	Robert Smith
Scenic Designer	Matthew M. Wehner
Lighting Designer	David Schmidt
Costume Designer	Amy L. Hutto
Sound Designer	John Stevens

SEED OF DARKNESS was produced courtesy of the Actors Equity Association at the Tamarind Theatre Los Angeles with the following cast:

EDGAR POE	George Jenesky
ELMIRA	Marjorie Harris
VIRGINIA	Katherine Armstrong
WHITMAN	Robin Harlan
MARY	Maxine John
MRS. ELIOT	Laura Leyva
GRISWOLD	Carl Bressler
BRIGGS	Wayne Heffley
INSPECTOR/ROYSTER	Frank Parker
DANNY	Joe Colligan
MRS. CLEMM	Gail Johnston
SHELTON/DEPUTY	Patrick Barrett
LAURIE/BLATHERSKITE #2	Lori King
BETH/LADY #1	Julie Pop
LADY #2/BLATHERSKITE #1	Beverly Christensen

Director	Ron Burrus
Producer	Conrad Dunn
Producer	Robin Harlan
Stage Manager	Peter Goldman
Costume Designer	Beverly Harlan
Lighting Designer	Richard Taylor

SEED OF DARKNESS
The Final Tale of Edgar Allan Poe

O, human love! thou spirit given
On Earth, of all we hope in Heaven!
-- E.A.P.

CHARACTERS

EDGAR ALLAN POE, poet

The Spectre of ELMIRA ROYSTER

VIRGINIA, the poet's wife
Sarah WHITMAN, the poet's mistress
MARY, a girl from his past
MRS. ELIOT, a woman in his present

The Reverend RUFUS GRISWOLD

CHARLES BRIGGS, editor

The INSPECTOR, Edward Mulhearn

DANNY PIPER, a constable

The following roles may be doubled:

BLATHERSKITE #1, friend to Mrs. Eliot
BLATHERSKITE #2, friend to Mrs. Eliot

MRS. CLEMM, Virginia's mother

ROYSTER, Elmira's Father
A. Barrett SHELTON, Elmira's betrothed

DEPUTY, Clell
LAURIE, prostitute
BETH, prostitute

FIRST WOMAN
SECOND WOMAN

ON STAGING

Throughout, Poe plays in and out of reality. During
memories he may be the passionate man of the scene, or a
detached onlooker participating in body only while his
mind remains rooted with Elmira in the ghostly present.

The simple stage furniture and dressings may be doubled
or implied. The couch of the Clemm household becomes
Poe's bed, the Journal's bench, and Whitman's bed.
Writing desks become kitchen tables and saloon bars.

Several scenes with ethereal Elmira may be played with
little more than spots illuminating the characters.

SETTING

New York, Fall 1849.

Also, the mind and memories of Edgar Allan Poe.

ACT ONE

ACT ONE

> Lights up on Edgar Allan Poe.

POE
Elmira?

> The spectre of Elmira Royster
> in a mirror.

ELMIRA
What have you done, Edgar?

> Lights down.
>
> Night. A street, 1849.
> Gas lamps. A saloon.
>
> Two Prostitutes, Beth and
> Laurie.
>
> A Rich Man enters.

BETH
What a purse! I've got him.

LAURIE
Have him choose for himself.

BETH
You got the last one.

LAURIE
He choosed me.

BETH
It's my turn.

> A Saloon Girl emerges and
> exits with the Rich Man.

BETH
Oh, my lord... it's been a bad night.

> Reverend Rufus Griswold
> enters, uncomfortable with
> the neighborhood.

BETH
Oh, no, Laurie, another one bearing salvation.

LAURIE
I had something worth saving once. Misplaced it at
thirteen years old.

BETH
I was twelve.

LAURIE
Just a child. Shame, shame.

BETH
Never saw the value. Commodity's only a commodity if you're trading it.

LAURIE
Couldn't be making a living if you'd kept it locked in a safe place! (laughs) Here he comes.

BETH
Looks like he's got it locked away so long he's forgotten he had it.

GRISWOLD
(stiff) Excuse me. Madame -- ?

LAURIE
-- not yet, sir, but I'm working my way up --

BETH
-- by working her way down --

GRISWOLD
I cannot approve of your means of living. However, there are certain missions suited to your character. I would employ you at this time. Could you -- ? Uh, would you perform a small favor?

LAURIE
Small or large, price is the same.

GRISWOLD
I'd be willing to pay.

LAURIE
Bet your ass.

GRISWOLD
(hands her a coin) I will not enter that establishment. Will you be so kind as to locate a friend for me? In the saloon?

LAURIE
They charge more in there to be your friend than we do out here.

GRISWOLD
No, no, I'm looking for a man.

BETH
Oh, my lord... it's been a bad night.

GRISWOLD
He should be fairly easy to pick out. He's a poet.

> Sardonic Poe enters, stumbling, balancing his cane.

POE
Harmony in an imperfect universe!

GRISWOLD
Poe! It's almost midnight, Briggs has sent me to this awful street to fetch you -- !

> Poe drinks from a bottle, drops the cane.

POE
-- however temporary. Bitch.

GRISWOLD
I would discuss the universe in your study. (sees bottle) What is that?

POE
Medicine, Griswold.

GRISWOLD
Opium.

POE
Laudanum. For the pain.

GRISWOLD
Are you ill?

POE
Wounded.

GRISWOLD
A fight?

POE
Worse.

GRISWOLD
Dueling again? Edgar?

POE
Yes.

GRISWOLD
Good God! Where were you touched?

POE
Here. (his heart) Don't look, Rufus, you shall find
nothing. Not on the surface. But inside, deep, buried, a
wound as real as she had parried my tender intentions and
riposted with a Russian rapier.

GRISWOLD
(realizing, sarcastic) And who was this exquisite fencer?

POE
One well-trained, I assure you.

GRISWOLD
I had no idea Sarah Whitman partakes of the sport.

POE
Her point is as true and deadly as an adder.

GRISWOLD
The night is cold, Edgar. And I have no self-pity with which to warm myself. Unhappily, it appears you have enough for us both.

LAURIE
(to Beth, re: Poe) A bit worn, but still a gentleman.

POE
Look at them, Rufus. Even their lowliness carries a terrible loveliness. What is it in them that makes a man's loins ache? I would understand the power they wield, or I fear I will go to my grave hating them for possessing it.

GRISWOLD
Though we are in agreement, our reasons differ; I despise them. Come along, Edgar, this is no place for men of our calibre.

POE
How would you know what my calibre is, Griswold? You're a goddamn reverend.

Prostitutes approach.

GRISWOLD
(to Poe) I will tell Mr. Briggs that I saw you. And that you were predisposed. (to Beth and Laurie) I pray God the world shall be rid of your kind. Quickly.

Griswold exits.

BETH
(to Poe) Share your bottle with a lady, sir?

POE
Goodnight, Reverend Griswold. "See you at the office."

LAURIE
Virgins... you can't trust 'em.

BETH
(hangs on Poe) It is very cold out, sir.

POE
I have dared the sands of the Sahara to drink the clouds of an Ethiope night.

BETH
Scary. Seventy-five cents.

POE
Following such an arduous journey... I want comforting.

BETH
(laughs) How long's it been?

LAURIE
If it be long enough, I'll do him for funnin'. Poor bargaining, sir, very poor. Never let the shopkeeper know you want the goods.

BETH
Water in a desert... very valuable.

LAURIE
Need rises. You rises. Price rises. One silver dollar to quench you.

POE
I am parched.

BETH
Well, he's honest. (to Poe) One-fifty.

POE
Ravenous.

BETH
Shrewd, too, I see. One and seventy-five. Erect an oasis.

POE
I can't be alone tonight.

LAURIE
Now, now, now. He's downright adorable. One-fifty. For the two of us. Together.

BETH
Laurie! That ain't businesswoman talk.

LAURIE
Keep a full dollar for yourself. I want his dark eyes.

BETH
Them? They make me shudder.

LAURIE
(smiles) Likewise.

BETH
Have to keep mine closed to keep his from looking inside.

LAURIE
(to Poe) What you say? Give a dollar and a half? A dollar?

BETH
(to Laurie) Take his marker why don't you?! Lend him the coin yourself. He ain't ope'd his mouth but twice and we're paying. Now that's a silly turn; imagine a wife putting out gold for the privilege of putting out in general. Whoaaa! (Poe stumbles, sits.)

> Constable Danny and a
> Deputy step up.

DANNY
Beth. Laurie. Let the gentleman be.

LAURIE
Danny! You're always bustin' up the fun without never tasting of it yourself.

> Laurie goes to kiss Danny's
> cheek. He grabs her hand.

LAURIE
A little boy, ain't you...

BETH
You're ruinin' his personal economy, Constable. He was about to make three or four dollar. (to Poe) How about that, mister? You charge your wife, or not?

POE
(drops his coins) My wife is dead.

BETH
(laughs) A sailor used that tale a week ago to try me for
nothing. It worked... except I carried off his money belt.
Weren't too hard after I got it unstrapped... and that was
easy in the first place --

> Stony faces from Poe and
> Laurie.

LAURIE
Beth.

BETH
You're telling the truth, ain't you. Oh, my lord... it's been a
bad night.

> Beth exits.
> Danny gestures and Deputy
> goes off after her.

LAURIE
(gathers Poe's fallen coins) Beth don't mean anything, Sir.

POE
Laurie. Thank you.

LAURIE
(kisses him on the cheek) Those eyes.

> She exits.
> Poe takes a drink.

DANNY
Go easy on that, Mr. Poe.

POE
Do I know you?

12

DANNY
I heard you speak once. Like your stories, too.

POE
Any poetry?

DANNY
I bought a copy of Tamerlane.

POE
Oh, you're the one.

DANNY
My chief, he likes your detective stories. He loved the way Inspector Dupin solved the Murders of the Rue Morgue. And the Parisian Prefect character, the chief considers him an idiot. Actually, he rather reminds me of the chief, himself. You ever hear of the fellow who borrows books and never returns them?

POE
Stealing a book is an evil second only to plagiarism. Behavior unbecoming of man or beast.

DANNY
Well, that's the chief. I loaned the bastard my copy of your collection. Haven't seen it since.

POE
The bastard.

DANNY
Don't say anything about me calling him that, will you?

POE
Would I take Chief Mulhearn into my confidence? He is a
bastard. I've known him since he was a constable like
yourself.

DANNY
Personally, or professionally, Mr. Poe?

POE
Professionally, I'm afraid. You see, young man, there are
certain freedoms of which I partake that I feel are above the
law. I tried to convince Mr. Mulhearn my feelings were
correct. He did not agree with my logic, and brought the
law, a badge, and a gun to his side of the argument.

DANNY
He jailed you.

POE
Yes.

DANNY
For exercising what "freedoms," sir?

POE
Drinking and dueling.

DANNY
(laughs) The law ain't always just, Mr. Poe.

POE
To your honesty. (drinks)

Deputy re-enters.

DEPUTY
She's bedded down. Uh, alone.

14

DANNY
Clell, this is Edgar Poe.

DEPUTY
You don't say. Well, Mr. Poe, Danny here likes your stories. Says they're short, though. Can't say I ever read any. I like real books. Always keep one in the outhouse, I do. Can read this much, when I'm constipated. How come you don't write any long books, Mr. Poe? Novels aren't your forte? ("fortay") On the other hand, maybe I should try one of your stories, I could finish the whole thing in a single visit to the pot! Ha, ha!

POE
Forte. (fort)

DEPUTY
What's that?

POE
Fort. Not "fortay." (drinks again)

DANNY
(the bottle) Best give that here, Mr. Poe.

DEPUTY
(angry) You don't want we should fine you.

POE
And you don't want I should bill you for a tutorial in pronunciation and grammar. Imbecile. (drinks)

DEPUTY
You snobby son of a bitch -- I'll box your ears -- ! (grabs Poe's lapel)

DANNY
-- leave him be. Clell! Let him go. (separates them) Go on home, Mr. Poe. Get some sleep.

POE
...sleep. Daniel, is it?

DANNY
Yes, sir, Mr. Poe.

POE
Edgar.

DANNY
Edgar, sir.

POE
Very good to have met you, Daniel.

> Poe ignores Deputy, then exits.

DEPUTY
(shouting after) It's best I haven't read you... probably use the pages to wipe myself!

DANNY
(cuffs the back of Deputy's head) The man deserves respect.

> They exit.
>
> The empty street.
>
> Laurie re-enters fixing her bodice.

16

A Cloaked Figure watches.

LAURIE
Give it a rest. I'm closed. (she recognizes the Figure) Oh, well, well. C'mon. Be a shame not to. Let's go, love.

> The Figure grabs her. Her giggling becomes sexual. A struggle. Her scream is silenced as the Figure brings a blade to her exposed throat.
>
> Blackout.
>
> Lights up.
>
> Poe alone in his bedroom.

POE
(drinks) Damnit... this stuff.

> He sleeps.
> Elmira's spectre in a ghostly light.

ELMIRA
What have you done, Edgar? What have you done?

> With a wave of her hand, Poe's bed becomes a couch in the Clemm household. Mrs. Clemm making juice.
>
> Young Virginia enters.

VIRGINIA
Mama -- mama! Jamie Cookson pulled my hair.

MRS. CLEMM
I'm sure you did something to deserve it.

VIRGINIA
Nothing, Mama. I promise.

MRS. CLEMM
Nothing? Then he must be quite taken with you.
Goddamn the springtime.

VIRGINIA
But, Mama --

MRS. CLEMM
Shush, your cousin is sleeping.

VIRGINIA
Eddy is here? Oh! (rushes to couch) Oh. He looks awful.
Is he sick? His breath smells like medicine.

MRS. CLEMM
Medicine, I doubt.

VIRGINIA
His clothes are wrinkled.

MRS. CLEMM
Got here after four this morning.

VIRGINIA
Was he burning the midnight oil? Yes! He was writing a
story, got to a stuck part, he told me he always gets to a
stuck part, then went walking to clear his head, got tired
and found himself in our neighborhood, and stopped to
sleep.

MRS. CLEMM
I'm not certain that's the way things went, Virginia. More than likely your cousin was burning the oil at one saloon after another, found himself miles from home, stopped to sleep, and got no work done at all.

VIRGINIA
Don't talk that way of Eddy. Look, here is a poem.

MRS. CLEMM
Probably something another writer gave to him to print.

VIRGINIA
(reads prim and properly, but with growing confusion)
Filled with mingled cream and amber, I will drain that glass again..."

MRS. CLEMM
Nope, that's our Eddy.

VIRGINIA
"...Such hilarious visions clamber Through the chamber of my brain -- Quaintest thoughts -- queerest fancies Come to life and fade away. What care I how time advances? I am drinking ale today." Hmmm. What does this mean, Mama?

MRS. CLEMM
Means we were both right. The boy never ceases to amaze me. Here. Give him this.

> Virginia crosses to Mrs. Clemm for glass of juice.
>
> Poe spies Virginia heading his way, and feigns sleep.

MRS. CLEMM
Careful. Don't spill it.

VIRGINIA
Oh, Mama. (she crosses to couch)

POE
Boo!

VIRGINIA
Aaaah! (the juice goes right in his face)

VIRGINIA
Oh, Eddy, oh. Here. (wipes his face with her skirt)

MRS. CLEMM
Not with your dress, Virginia.

POE
It's all right, Sissy. I'm all right.

VIRGINIA
You scared me.

POE
If only "Spirits of the Dead" would do the same for the reading public. (wipes his face on page)

VIRGINIA
No, Eddy, not on that.

POE
(reads) Fill with mingled cream and amber... What's this?

VIRGINIA
Why, that's your poem.

POE
You're certain?

VIRGINIA
It is your handwriting.

POE
Ha! Fantastic! "What care I how time advances? I am drinking ale today!" (laughs, holds head) Ooh, a bit too much, I'm afraid, my head hurts.

VIRGINIA
(massages his temples) Is that better?

POE
That feels wonderful, Virginia. I must visit you and your mother more often.

VIRGINIA
We'd like that. Very much.

POE
I'm so busy now. In my work, I really must make time.

VIRGINIA
You were busy in your work last night?

POE
(off Mrs. Clemm's look) No, I -- I, I promise to visit more often, Sissy. Every week.

VIRGINIA
(sits on his lap) Where did you go last night?

POE
Um, to a party.

VIRGINIA
Who was the party for?

POE
Well, it wasn't for anyone or anything in particular.

VIRGINIA
Where was it?

POE
It was a place where people go to have a party.

VIRGINIA
Did you know everyone?

POE
No.

VIRGINIA
Did you know anyone?

POE
Not at first.

VIRGINIA
Then they were strangers?

POE
Yes.

VIRGINIA
So it was at a place where people go who have no reason for a party, but who want to have the fun of a party.

MRS. CLEMM
Don't look at me, Eddy.

POE
Yes, Virginia... you've hit it.

VIRGINIA
How do you get an invitation to the party if the person giving the party is a stranger to you?

POE
Anyone may come. Everyone's invited.

VIRGINIA
Then you will take me next time?

POE
No.

VIRGINIA
Why not?

POE
Because the people who own the place where the party is won't allow young ladies in.

VIRGINIA
Was there dancing?

POE
People were dancing.

VIRGINIA
Did you dance?

POE
Uh, yes.

VIRGINIA
If there were no ladies there, how did you dance?

MRS. CLEMM
There is a certain kind of woman, Virginia, who you can't rightly call a lady.

POE
Thank you, Muddy.

VIRGINIA
Did you dance with Elmira?

POE
Elmira doesn't take well to such places.

VIRGINIA
Will you dance with me, Eddy? Now?

POE
Sissy, my head hurts.

VIRGINIA
But you dance with your feet. Come on.

POE
(rising, groaning) Ohh, whoa.

MRS. CLEMM
Still at arms with your mingled cream and amber?

POE
Losing the battle, I'm afraid.

VIRGINIA
Here. (forces him up)

POE
Oww. Last time we did this you came no higher than my
middle vest button. Look how you've grown.

VIRGINIA
Go.

POE
Of course.

> They dance playfully.

> Mrs. Clemm exits.

VIRGINIA
What kind of place were you dancing in?

POE
A banquet room.

VIRGINIA
Mama said you were in a saloon.

POE
Your mother's a very smart lady.

VIRGINIA
When I'm older, Eddy, is there a place we can dance?

POE
Someday, at the music hall.

VIRGINIA
In celebration of a great event!

POE
A holiday? Christmas?

VIRGINIA
No. It must be something special for you.

POE
I'll tell you what... you and I will dance when Elmira and I are married. At the reception!

VIRGINIA
No. I know; when a poem you write makes you rich!

POE
We may be too old to dance at all by then.

VIRGINIA
All the beautiful couples will be there. Important people. Pretty ladies with their husbands. Young men with their fiancés. All dancing happily. You will bring me, Eddy. Please?

POE
Yes, Sissy.

VIRGINIA
So you will be my beau? Say yes, Eddy.

POE
(laughing) I already have a girl.

VIRGINIA
Elmira?

POE
Yes.

VIRGINIA
But she doesn't love you like I do, Eddy. Besides, I've
known you longer. (Poe laughs) All right, I'll let you dance
once or twice with Elmira, but you must be mine all the
other times.

POE
What, and leave the handsome young man who
accompanies you to the advances of other pretty girls?

VIRGINIA
What young man? There will be no one else.

POE
Oh, Sissy, there will be many men. Boys will watch you
from blocks away trying to muster courage to speak with
you. Soldiers in proper dress will see your beauty and
proudly stumble over themselves to fall in your good grace.
Older men would try their hand and promise the devil their
souls if he would make them young again for a moment in
your eyes, for in those eyes will sit judgment itself; all fear
and hope weighed by your look. There will be many men,
indeed, Virginia, each doing his damndest to win your
heart.

VIRGINIA
I've already given it away. They'll be too late.

POE
Oh, no Sissy. (laughing) No, no.

> He hugs her, playfully. Not
> taking her seriously.

VIRGINIA
I don't care who they are.

POE
You'll feel differently.

VIRGINIA
No, I won't. I mean that, Eddy! (she breaks away) Don't
laugh. Don't! Of everything in the world, Eddy, I wish I
was Elmira Royster so we could be together always.

> Virginia exits.
> Mrs. Clemm enters with a
> bottle.

MRS. CLEMM
What's the matter, Edgar?

POE
I was thinking.

MRS. CLEMM
A habit of yours. You really got to stop.

POE
It's a shame she must grow up.

MRS. CLEMM
Virginia? Oh, Edgar, who would want to stay a child
forever? I look forward to the day she sees the world
through older eyes.

POE
You're a unique woman, Muddy. Most do not wish their
children to experience such clarity. Truth is often ugly.

MRS. CLEMM
(looking in mirror) Often fairly damned good-looking,
too, if I do say so myself. Now what you thinkin'?

POE
Virginia. She'll make someone very happy someday.

MRS. CLEMM
Only a fool wouldn't be happy with my Virginia.

> Mrs. Clemm exits.

ELMIRA
What have you done, Edgar?

> Lights down on the Clemm home.
>
> Lights up on Poe, sits up in bed. Shaking.
>
> Elmira exits like a shadow.

POE
Elmira? Elmira? Oh, God.

> Lights up.
> Newspaper office.
>
> Griswold and editor Briggs discuss a manuscript.

BRIGGS
-- Poe handles this sort of thing. I have little knowledge of it.

GRISWOLD
You are the editor.

BRIGGS
This is a poem, Rufus. I pay Edgar Poe four hundred
dollars a year to select, critique, and edit such submissions.
I appreciate your compassion in taking this young poet,
this (reads) "Master Sidney Wolrige," under your wing.
Perhaps we shall publish this verse of his. Perhaps not.
However, since Poe has been literary editor here,
subscriptions have trebled. He will make the final
decision. That is his talent. That is his function.

GRISWOLD
(Poe's vacant desk) Of what use is talent, if its possessor is
not present to exercise it in the performance of his
function?

BRIGGS
(clears throat) Where is your religious column, Rufus?

GRISWOLD
I'll fetch it.

BRIGGS
Good. I believe I have reserved an entire half page.
Adequate space for more than a week's worth of righteous
indignation. (dons a coat) I'll be at lunch. Leave the
poem. Poe shall look at it when -- whenever he gets in.

GRISWOLD
I'd rather he read it while I am in the room... so that I may
take his criticisms back to -- uh, Wolrige.

BRIGGS
Leave the poem, Rufus.

GRISWOLD
Yes, sir.

> Griswold exits.

BRIGGS
Sanctimonious popinjay.

> Poe enters, head throbbing.

BRIGGS
Poe!

POE
Charles. Shhhh.

BRIGGS
I would invite you to lunch, but, as our good reverend has indicated, you have been absent from your desk all morning and have a great deal of work ahead of you.

> Poe places pages on desk.

BRIGGS
Good God, Edgar, you look dreadful. If you're ill you should have stayed home. (sees pages) What's this?

POE
Seven pages of marginalia, critiques of three poems by two would-be Boston poets, an article on the daft thousands heading for California to sift their fortunes from the dirt, and a short-story.

BRIGGS
The Cask of Amontillado.

POE
"Amontiyado."

BRIGGS
Whichever. "The thousand injuries of Fortunato I had borne as best I could; but when he ventured upon insult, I vowed revenge." Oh, God, Poe, another horror tale?

POE
The hero in this story has his reasons for behaving "horribly." For those who have been put upon, it illustrates a most pleasant and thorough revenge. And for those who have done the putting, it serves as gleeful terror. Readers of either school will find use for the story... and buy more copies of your newspaper.

BRIGGS
You completed these this morning?

POE
The true portrait of a man may be observed in his ability to work with a hangover.

BRIGGS
Then, I have never laid eyes on a more masculine picture, Edgar. Ha. And what have we here? (a single scrap) "Sarah Whitman. Three-fifteen Diamond Lane."

POE
(taking address) I gathered all piled on my nightstand. That apparently fell in.

BRIGGS
Mrs. Whitman has moved again, has she, Poe? I'd say she's trying to hide from you, if I didn't know any better. Not very good at it anyway; four different residences in a year, and she always manages for you to learn her whereabouts. She fears you, but she wants you. How did she arrange to have you find her this time?

POE
She took a classified with this Journal. This is the billing address.

BRIGGS
Selling?

POE
A "spare trunk of men's clothing, size forty."

BRIGGS
Your clothes! Ha! She'll be sorry if she sells them. She doesn't mean to be rid of you. Not really. What price is she asking?

POE
An exorbitant one.

BRIGGS
I knew it! She means to keep them around to fire the scorching memories of her rutting Edgar, or to have something warm to dress you in when you come begging for the shelter of her home and bosom on a rainy night. Not that there aren't other bosoms upon which you may rest your weary head... Christ, Edgar, how does a man with a desk as disheveled as yours keep on track so many women? You're like a switchman in a rail yard! Ha, ha. Come, my friend, let's have a bath, new suits of clothes. I'm a fifty-two and I'll wager you're a size forty. Then, some lunch. I'm starving, and Mrs. Sheila is serving liver pie.

POE
(the hangover) Ohhhhh --

BRIGGS
Well, if you'd rather not. Have a look at this then. (Poe
reads) A poem by a Sidney Wolrige. Griswold brought it
in. He hopes for a commission, I think. Shall we publish
it?

POE
(grabbing scissors and paste) Not in its present form.

> Griswold enters to see
> scissors and pen flying as Poe
> quickly cuts and pastes the
> poem.

POE
Yes.

GRISWOLD
You have omitted an entire stanza!

BRIGGS
An improvement, would you agree?

GRISWOLD
Yes. Yes, indeed.

BRIGGS
If Wolrige will allow, we shall print this rendition. Rufus?

GRISWOLD
I'm sure he will.

BRIGGS
Best check with him first.

GRISWOLD
I am authorized to -- speak in his behalf.

BRIGGS
Good. I'm off to lunch.

Briggs exits.

POE
By his enthusiasm, this Wolrige shows to be a good prospect. His skill, however, is lacking; both the subject and execution show a sort of... constipation. Not to offend him, my additions and deletions were obvious trifles.

GRISWOLD
Not so obvious --

POE
-- a more seasoned professional would have readily observed the blunders, and altered before submitting --

GRISWOLD
-- the poem is mine, Edgar.

POE
Oh. Dear friend.

GRISWOLD
I shall continue compiling the works of others, rather than composing my own.

POE
Nonsense. Ability grows with practice. There is nothing magical about writing; this is a job of work, Rufus.

GRISWOLD
You execute it with ease.

POE
(no) I wrote The Raven with a hundred deliberate steps.
(pause) Melancholy is the most legitimate of tones. I
pondered for weeks to discover the most dispirited of
English words. (Griswold waits) "Nevermore."

GRISWOLD
Ah.

POE
Ah. And the most melancholy of topics?

GRISWOLD
Death?

POE
Of course. (Griswold proud!) If it allies itself with beauty.
Therefore, the death of a beautiful woman is
unquestionably the most poetical topic in the world.

GRISWOLD
The art is clinical.

POE
Still, I would not have been successful in the execution had
I not actually felt the pain myself... in the past.

GRISWOLD
Oh, Poe. You were writing of poor Virginia all the while.

POE
No. I wrote the poem while my wife lived. Years before I
was wed to Virginia, I was engaged to another. It is the loss
of her, whom the student in The Raven mourns. The Fall of
my seventeenth year, I had been away at university. I
returned home at Christmastime with one desire; to hold in
my arms my beloved, Elmira...

> Light change.
>
> The porch of the Royster
> mansion. Christmas tunes
> sung behind.
>
> Elmira enters, not a spectre,
> but a lively and wise eighteen
> year old.

POE
I beg you... reconsider.

ELMIRA
It is too late.

> Royster, Elmira's prosperous
> father, enters.

ROYSTER
Hurry in, Elmira. Barrett is waiting at the piano. Hello,
Edgar.

POE
Waiting? How long?

ELMIRA
Don't --

ROYSTER
Too long, I'm afraid. Can't expect him to wait forever.

POE
Forever? Your relatives haven't sung but two weepy carols since Elmira and I stepped out. Why does it surprise me that your daughter couldn't wait a single semester for me? Must seem like an eternity to anyone in your family. True to their word for the better part of a clock tick or they're unworthy of the name Royster.

ELMIRA
Edgar!

ROYSTER
Your fiancé awaits you, Elmira.

POE
At the piano -- fa la la la la.

ROYSTER
I know your father --

POE
-- Stepfather.

ROYSTER
True, you've none of his blood in you.

POE
You're two of a kind.

ROYSTER
John Allan is a decent hardworking man.

POE
A lecherous fool.

ROYSTER
You are not worthy of his unending patience.

POE
A fart who fears five minutes is forever lectures me on patience? I've been away for all of Autumn, sweating in books of Latin, mathematics, and, god forbid, nineteenth century etiquette, living for the day I could return to Elmira, and you tell me how patient my father is? How patient you are? The Royster Christmas ham is getting cold, man, better hurry in for your slice before it spoils; a veritable millennium has passed since the Misses yanked it from the stove two hours ago!

ROYSTER
You insolent boy --

POE
-- This boy would call you out, sir.

ELMIRA
Edgar! Don't mock my father. (steps between them) No. Father, go inside. I'll follow right in. Please.

> A. Barrett Shelton, 18, proper
> wimp, steps onto porch.

SHELTON
Everything all right, Mr. Royster? Elmy?

POE
"Elmy?" Good God.

ELMIRA
Get inside. Both of you. I'm all right.

SHELTON
Very well. (touches Elmira's hand) I've composed a carol for you.

> Royster leads Shelton into house.

ROYSTER
(to Shelton) I think it's time you stopped addressing me as Mr. Royster, young man. You'll be part of the family soon.

> They exit.

POE
And the moments will be centuries, Shelton. The gatherings will last forever; a taste of hell with your helping of poultry and bread pudding. Why are you smiling?

ELMIRA
You never stop.

POE
I want you. I have never stopped wanting you.

ELMIRA
I'm engaged to Barrett now.

POE
Not yet married.

ELMIRA
(weakening) Not yet.

POE
Then there is hope.

ELMIRA
No, Edgar. Not for you and me. I will miss you.

POE
(desperate) Come to the university with me.

ELMIRA
No talk like that.

POE
We could live in town. You could --

ELMIRA
-- Barrett is a fine man. I've given my word to him.

POE
What of your word to me?

ELMIRA
I kept your letters.

SHELTON
(off) Elmy?

ELMIRA
-- both of them.

POE
Both? What?

SHELTON
(off) Elmy.

ELMIRA
-- but when you stopped writing --

POE
I never stopped... I wrote to you every day.

ROYSTER
(off) Elmira?

ELMIRA
-- I didn't hear from you for three months --

POE
I wrote a hundred letters!

ELMIRA
-- how could you expect me to wait when you gave no indication that you were true to me?

POE
Not true?

ELMIRA
I loved you Eddy. You broke my heart.

POE
No...

ELMIRA
Father saw my pain.

POE
(realizing) He kept my letters from you!

ELMIRA
(exiting) He arranged for me to meet Barrett. Gentle Barrett.

POE
I wrote a hundred times. Wait! No! I lost you!

> Young Elmira exits.
>
> Lights up on Poe and
> Griswold.

POE
I lost her. I have spent the better part of two decades
fathoming the nature of my misery. No matter. It is from
my melancholy, this personal knowledge, that I drew
substance to breathe life into the poem. You, Rufus, must
have the courage to bare your soul in the work, even if the
subject of the verse is death in life.

GRISWOLD
I'd rather be healthy and happy than hold onto a hard
memory for poetry's sake.

POE
Figures.

> Poe edits the newspaper.
> Griswold's questions are
> unwelcome interruptions.

GRISWOLD
Lenore is the personification of Elmira?

POE
Very good, Rufus. You'll be a poet, yet.

GRISWOLD
Elmira... Elmira Shelton.

POE
She was Elmira Royster when we were engaged.

GRISWOLD
But, I know her, Poe. As I know her husband, A. Barrett
Shelton. They are both very much alive in Richmond --

POE
-- don't speak of such things!

GRISWOLD
(pause, then quickly) He is a fine man. A hard-working
merchant. In transportation, too. Very successful.

POE
Rufus, when I fear my spirit has hit rock bottom, you have a
knack for tunneling me through the stone to a new and
deeper despair. Thank you for the allowing me to view the
very mantle of melancholy!

GRISWOLD
(pause) In The Raven, she was dead.

POE
(angry) If she is not here, if she is married to another, if
there is no hope that she shall ever return to me -- what is
the difference to my heart, soul, or body, between her living
a hundred miles away, or her being dead altogether!

GRISWOLD
It makes quite a difference to her, I imagine. And to Mr.
Shelton, as well.

POE
Rufus --

GRISWOLD
-- You should be pleased to learn she prospers.

POE
You're not making me feel any better.

GRISWOLD
Poe, if your heart is torn over Elmira, why would you choose to name the dead lover in the verse "Lenore?"

POE
Because... it rhymes... with Nevermore.

GRISWOLD
My brain hurts.

POE
Growing pains.

> A knock. Griswold sets the wet reworked poem on a chair and crosses to answer.

GRISWOLD
I fear I will never be a poet.

POE
(aside) Your fear is the world's hope. (knock) In the middle of a literary question, a five o'clock deadline, and the general populace feels it necessary to rap upon the editor's door.

> Griswold opens. The Inspector enters with Danny. The animosity between Poe and the Inspector is visible.

GRISWOLD
Good afternoon. Hello.

INSPECTOR
Gentlemen. Edward Mulhearn, Chief Inspector. This is my
deputy, Constable Daniel Piper.

GRISWOLD
I am the Reverend Rufus Griswold. Edgar Poe, assistant
editor.

POE
A very busy assistant editor. Hello, Inspector.

INSPECTOR
It's been some time, Mr. Poe. In an effort to understand
the human mind and its idiosyncrasies, I have acquainted
myself with some of your work.

POE
I understand you have a rather voluminous library, and ever
expanding. (winks to Danny)

DANNY
Hello, Mr. Poe.

POE
Hello, Daniel.

DANNY
(fingers "Amontillado") Is this a new story?

POE
Yes.

DANNY
Horror, revenge?

POE
Depends upon your point of view.

DANNY
May I?

POE
Certainly.

> Danny smiles and reads. His
> attention switching between
> the story and conversation.

INSPECTOR
(sitting on chair with cut and pasted poem) If you don't
mind my asking, Mr. Poe, why in your stories of detection
is the chief of the Parisian police always portrayed as the
fool?

POE
Personal experience.

INSPECTOR
Then you've been to Paris?

POE
No.

INSPECTOR
I resent the implication. (stands, paper stuck to his
trousers) I believe my system a watershed to the science of
criminal investigation. Utilizing my enormous capacity for
the understanding of human nature, I interview suspects
and gather from their characters what has proved to be the
final and most important piece of the investigative puzzle...
the intangible. It is my forte. (fortay)

POE
(cringing) You are one in a thousand. However, observe the ordinary as well as the intangible if you wish to learn the whole truth.

INSPECTOR
I regret that I come today in my professional capacity.

POE
As we are hurrying to make a deadline, and you, doubtlessly have several bad men to track, your visit would be a goddamn waste of time otherwise.

GRISWOLD
Poe!

POE
The good reverend... ever striving to save my soul.

INSPECTOR
We all need a bit of salvation now and again.

POE
Griswold feels I need it again and again.

GRISWOLD
That's not true, Poe. Take last night. I did not endeavor, well, perhaps mildly, to keep you from that... er... your business.

POE
Rufus --

INSPECTOR
-- Please continue, Reverend.

GRISWOLD
Well, last night --

POE
Is your business with The Journal, the Reverend, or myself?

INSPECTOR
My business is with you, Mr. Poe.

POE
Be quick, please. What sort?

GRISWOLD
Perhaps a paternity suit, Edgar? Ha, ha... No.

INSPECTOR
A woman was killed last night. Murdered. The second victim in a week. Both by the same hand.

POE
When was the first?

INSPECTOR
Friday, a widow was murdered.

POE
Are you aware of this, Rufus? Nor am I. In your crusade for the fathoming of human character, the obvious has escaped you, Inspector. This is a newspaper; why is it we were not informed?

INSPECTOR
I had my reasons for keeping you, and the public, in the dark. Certain evidence uncovered by my men led to the hush hush nature of the killing.

POE
Your hush-hushness may have cost that second woman her
life; she might have taken precautions and prevented her
own demise.

INSPECTOR
That is the very reason I must engage you and The Journal
now. This is the report on the first victim. It will show you
why the crime was kept secret and why your presence is
now required.

Poe is stunned by report.

GRISWOLD
What is it? Poe?

POE
Am I a suspect?

INSPECTOR
You were not. Not on the first murder. However, certain
evidence and witnesses now serve to make you one of
several suspected for the second and, therefore, also the
first.

GRISWOLD
What evidence? What does the report say?

INSPECTOR
The first victim was a Mrs. Mary Franklin --

DANNY
-- Frankville --

INSPECTOR
-- Frankville, formerly Mary Capel. (difficult, he really cares) That which made the crime unreportable was the condition of the corpse. Her throat was slit from ear to ear, through to the spine. Her face grossly disfigured. Breasts and other female parts were severed... some removed altogether. Mr. Poe's suggestion, that had I made the public aware of the murder subsequent ones may have been prevented, is true. However, I feared the hideous facts of the crime may have instigated a more costly vigilante panic. It was my hope the killing was a one-time occurrence. I was wrong. And will have to live with my decision.

POE
Poor Mary.

GRISWOLD
Did you know her, Poe?

INSPECTOR
I'm told she was beautiful... before.

POE
She was magnificent.

                    Saloon music.

                    Lights up on Mary.

MARY
You been looking at me.

POE
Pardon?

MARY
All night, you been looking at me. Why?

POE
Actually, no, I --

MARY
-- You stare out the window and pretend to look to the
street, but what you're really doing is either looking at me
dance in the reflection, or you're tryin' to be different than
the others by not noticing me and my new dress.
Therefore, you're looking even more than the rest 'cause
you're using your brains, too... not just that part. Can I sit
with you?

POE
But your gentlemen friends -- ?

MARY
Don't worry about them. Fine lads, really. But they lack --
well, let me say that tonight's not their night.

POE
And it is my night.

MARY
Could be. Buy me a drink. So, which is it? Were you
looking out trying to see my reflection, or were you just
pretending you weren't noticing?

POE
I was not watching your reflection.

MARY
Then you're sly.

POE
Neither was I pretending not to notice you.

MARY
Honest? Well, then I'll pay.

POE
No, no --

MARY
-- An investment it my future.

POE
Investment?

MARY
The first man who's rich enough to buy me, but has spine enough to keep from wetting himself in the process. I know how the world runs. I don't like to do work, sweating, sewing, washing, keeping books, that's what normal girls do. I got the assets that say I deserve better and don't have to do what's common... I got this uncommon face and this perfect bust. Beautiful, don't you think?

POE
Certainly.

MARY
Well, being my selling points, and being the only ones, I got to spend time painting them. I been shopping for the rightest buyer. I only get a single chance, and I want the best.

POE
You search for a husband to support you.

MARY
Oh, yes, but he's got to keep his dignity while doin' it.

POE
You're honesty is refreshing... disturbingly so.

MARY
(reaches in his trouser pocket) What's this? (a skeleton key)

POE
The key to my bedchamber door.

MARY
I'll believe that when I see you open it. Click, click! (they laugh) Show me. (they walk, her arm in his) Oh, lucky lucky you, Mr. Edgar Poe. I'm afraid I'm a bit drunk. Shhh. Does my face look flushed?

POE
It looks like --

MARY
-- fine marble.

POE
Yes.

MARY
You have a moustache. Very appealing. (a giggle becomes a kiss) Mmmm. (she leads him onward) You know, I can tell you come from an aristocratic family.

POE
How?

MARY
By the way you talk. Your confident arrogance. I would guess you are probably from the South.

POE
Your insight is amazing.

MARY
I've been around.

POE
I believe you.

MARY
Are the Poes well known in the South?

POE
Actually, no. My stepfather's name was Allan. I was adopted.

MARY
Nothing wrong with that. One could say I'm looking to get myself adopted, too. He's rich?

POE
Oh, yes.

MARY
Tobacco? Cotton?

POE
He's a merchant.

MARY
How lucky for you to have been taken in by such a man. Are you a merchant, too?

POE
No. I am engaged in the most sacred of endeavors: I am an author.

MARY
(brightening) Famous?

POE
My work has not yet found its audience.

MARY
You are wealthy, aren't you?

POE
I said my work has not been widely published.

MARY
(pause) Oh, lordy, you're a struggling writer.

POE
Uh, yes.

MARY
God, not another one! I thought you were rich.

POE
That was a conclusion you extrapolated.

MARY
Well, do you plan to be rich soon? When will they publish your novel?

POE
I write poetry.

MARY
There's no such thing as a rich poet! You should be ashamed for leading me on so. (sees "house") This is a boarding house!

POE
Mrs. Van Kamp doesn't mind visitors, but we must be quiet.

MARY
I'm not going in there. I thought you'd have a mansion. A house with servants, at least. Now I learn that you probably are a servant. I don't mean to offend you, Mr. Poe. You are very handsome, extremely witty, but I simply can't be with a poor man. I think that we should keep our relationship, um, platonic. Yes, that's the word, I think we should be friends and friends only.

POE
I could never have a platonic relationship with you.

MARY
Well, very well, then. I'll see you perhaps. Perhaps not. I must be going. Have you any money for a coach? Of course not. No need to walk me, I'll do all right. I wonder if Frankville is still awake?

> Mary exits.

> Newspaper Office.

POE
And I didn't see her again for some years.

DANNY
From the sound of her, you should count yourself the lucky one, Mr. Poe.

INSPECTOR
Daniel!

DANNY
I apologize. Forgive me.

GRISWOLD
Who is the second victim?

INSPECTOR
A prostitute. (hands Poe report)

GRISWOLD
The lowest of God's creatures and therefore most
deserving.

INSPECTOR
One Laurie Mulligan.

DANNY
Mullen, sir. Laurie Mullen.

GRISWOLD
Poe, last night... perhaps she was -- ?

POE
(remembering) Oh, Rufus, yes.

GRISWOLD
Dear God. But truly, you can't suspect Poe.

INSPECTOR
He was seen with the woman less than an hour before her
death.

GRISWOLD
But that's not ground for suspicion. Why I was with her
myself... not five minutes... before... P-Poe. Now,
Inspector, surely you don't suspect me -- I have an alibi --I -
- leading choir practice -- I -- !

INSPECTOR
Reverend -- Reverend -- Reverend, you may count yourself in considerable company... we have no less than four or six other men who were seen with her last night, and ten more who were with her on a somewhat regular basis during the past weeks.

GRISWOLD
Four, six, ten. My, the devil is industrious.

INSPECTOR
So is our killer. He slashed her more thoroughly than Mary Frankville. The doctor estimates, by her height and frame that Laurie Mulligan --

DANNY
-- Mullen, sir.

INSPECTOR
Yes. That she weighed more than a hundred and five pounds. The corpse weighed only ninety.

DANNY
Killer made off with about fifteen pounds of her.

GRISWOLD
Oh, my --

INSPECTOR
Her teeth were missing, Mr. Poe. Yanked.

GRISWOLD
What sort of a monster would so much as think of such a thing?

POE
I am such a monster, Rufus. The wife in my story Berenice
was molested in her grave... her teeth extracted by her
obsessed husband.

INSPECTOR
It is our wish, Mr. Poe, that these murders now be made
public. In your newspaper. However, and this is where I
require your cooperation for you may deny my will, I wish
you would say only that the two women were murdered, in
a like fashion, apparently by the same man, but do not give
any details that would cause undue fear; such publicity
could actually glorify this slasher and inspire a
continuation of the killings. The threat of death alone is
sufficient for the women in town to take precautions.

POE
I shall consult with Mr. Briggs, but I assure you we will do
as you wish.

INSPECTOR
Thank you. (dons hat) Well, we have other interviews.
Come along, Daniel.

DANNY
Inspector.

INSPECTOR
Yes, Constable?

DANNY
What about -- ?

INSPECTOR
-- Daniel.

DANNY
The man has to know. It's not right leaving him without.

INSPECTOR
We'll speak of this while we ride.

DANNY
No, sir. It's not fair to him. I've known him only a short time, but Mr. Poe is a fine man, suspect or not.

POE
What are you talking about?

DANNY
It can't hurt the investigation. I mean, him knowing... he has a right, Inspector.

INSPECTOR
Correct, Constable. Mr. Poe, the killer has left a sort of calling card with each murder. (searching his note pad) The one found on Mary reads, "O, feast my soul revenge is sweet, Temptress, take my scorn, Curs'd was the hour that saw us meet, The hour when we were born."

GRISWOLD
Poe, a rewording of your "Rise Infernal Spirits."

POE
Proceed.

INSPECTOR
And last night, the missing teeth of the harlot were only a part of the indication --

POE
-- read it.

INSPECTOR
"The impulse increases to a wish, the wish to an uncontrollable longing, and in defiance of all consequences, is indulged."

POE
"The Imp of the Perverse."

INSPECTOR
You won't print these details in the Journal?

POE
No.

INSPECTOR
Good. All we need at the station are a hundred letters from as many maniacs making claim to the foul deeds and signing their "confessions" with quotes from your work. Might boost your sales some, eh?

POE
God damn you, man. Get out of my sight.

INSPECTOR
I thank you for your cooperation.

> Griswold ushers the
> Inspector out. They exit.

DANNY
I'm sorry about all this, Mr. Poe. When we catch him, I'll thrash him a good one for you.

POE
Daniel. What makes you think I am not the man you seek?

DANNY
Cause, Mr. Poe. The man we're looking for has so much hatred in him he has to kill. Hates women and got no way to get the hatred out. You might have some contempt, but you... you write. Sort of purge yourself. It's the fellow who's got something to fight, but can't find a way of getting it out that worries me. Your pain leads you to writing. His leads him to the killing. Hell, the bastard should've taken up the rodeo or something. The town'd be better off, not to mention the two ladies. Good day, Mr. Poe.

> Danny exits.
>
> Elmira's Specter enters.

ELMIRA
What have you done, Edgar?

POE
Leave me alone, damn you.

ELMIRA
Two women were killed.

POE
Don't add guilt to my sorrow. I was true to you. I could never love another. Never.

> Elmira gestures. A memory
> of Mrs. Clemm adjusting
> Virginia's bridal dress.

VIRGINIA
It's so pretty.

MRS. CLEMM
I wore this dress when I married your father.

POE
Virginia!

VIRGINIA
It makes me look older, do you think?

MRS. CLEMM
Don't you worry about such things.

VIRGINIA
Did you see Eddy in his coat? He looks so serious... so handsome.

MRS. CLEMM
Oh, I'll be damned.

VIRGINIA
Mother.

MRS. CLEMM
That's my bust, you know. You're fourteen years old and this bodice is too small. You're definitely a woman. And your cousin is a good man, Virginia; I pray he keeps you fat with Eastern beef and Southern babies!

VIRGINIA
One boy and one girl.

MRS. CLEMM
Think bigger, darling. Better to have four --

VIRGINIA
All right... two boys and two girls.

MRS. CLEMM
-- four of each.

VIRGINIA
Eight children! Yes! And proud of their daddy.

> Poe steps beside her.
> Griswold enters to perform
> wedding ceremony.

POE
(to Spectre, re: Virginia) She's beautiful.

ELMIRA
She adores you, Edgar.

GRISWOLD
-- in according to the ordinance of God, in the holy bond of marriage?

VIRGINIA
I will.

ELMIRA
She loves you.

GRISWOLD
Edgar, wilt thou have this woman to be thy wife --

ELMIRA
Thy wife.

GRISWOLD
-- and wilt thou pledge thy troth to her, in all love --

ELMIRA
In all love.

POE
(to Spectre) I wrote a hundred letters.

GRISWOLD
-- to comfort each other in sickness, trouble, and sorrow --

ELMIRA
In sickness.

GRISWOLD
-- and to live together according to the ordinance of God, in the holy bond of marriage?

ELMIRA
I will, Edgar?

POE
(facing Virginia) I will, Elmira.

GRISWOLD
By the authority committed unto me, I declare that Edgar and Virginia are now husband and wife.

ELMIRA
'Til death do you part.

> Virginia engages Poe in
> wedding kiss.

ELMIRA
"I'll never love another. I could not. I cannot."

POE
It is true, Elmira. It is true.

ELMIRA
Then it is a shame!

> Blackout.

> Night. Street lamps.
> Two Women enter.

FIRST WOMAN
Congratulations, Michelle. Very good work.

SECOND WOMAN
I couldn't have done it without you; it takes many hands to keep the accounts. I'm exhausted. Oh, I catch my carriage here.

FIRST WOMAN
I'll wait with you.

SECOND WOMAN
Nonsense. Your aching back and your lonely husband call you to bed.

FIRST WOMAN
You shouldn't wait alone. Not with a lunatic lurking about.

SECOND WOMAN
He's no more dangerous than my Abraham, I assure you. And I have this. (a derringer)

FIRST WOMAN
Well, then. Here, let me give you your papers. Goodnight, Michelle. Same time tomorrow?

> First Woman exits.

SECOND WOMAN
Bright and early.

> Second Woman waits.
>
> The Figure enters, she turns,
> he brings the knife down.
>
> Blackout.
>
> The sound of the derringer
> shot in the darkness.

END OF ACT ONE

ILLUSTRATIONS

Edgar Allan Poe

**Virginia Poe
by G.G. Learned**

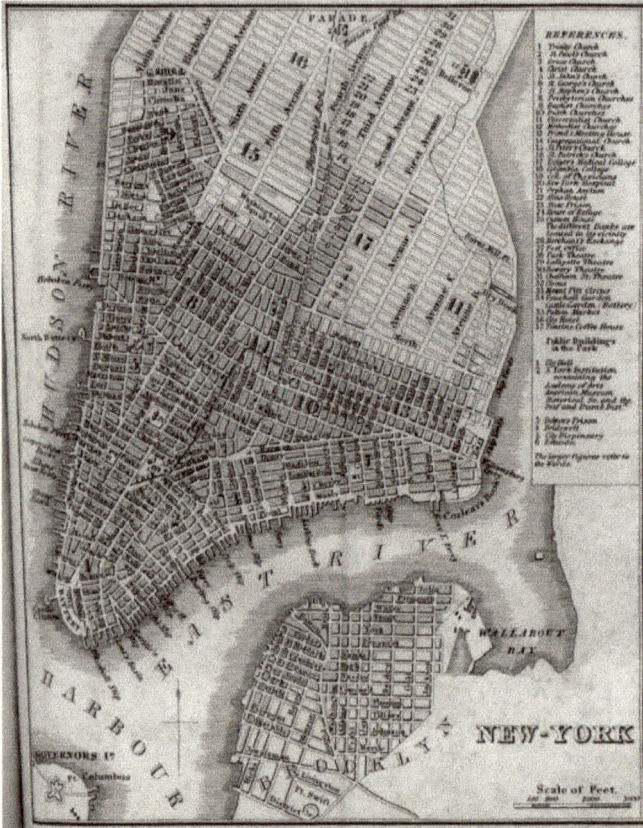

New York City, circa 1849

Virginia's Romantic Rival, Poe, Virginia
from Graham's Fashion Plates

Poe Cottage, The Bronx
where Virginia died

Virginia Poe
second portrait by Thomas Sully

Sarah Helen Whitman

Reverend Rufus Griswold

Elmira Royster

Mrs. Clemm
Virginia's Mother

Virginia Poe
deathbed watercolor

Edgar Allan Poe

ACT TWO

ACT TWO

Night.

Poe knocks.

A pretty Woman in her
thirties answers.

WOMAN
Hello.

POE
I hope I haven't disturbed you.

WOMAN
I am hours from retiring.

POE
Most would be asleep by now.

WOMAN
(sarcastic) I have a fascination for the nighttime. I prefer
shadows and shapes painted by moonlight and blackness,
to the harsh opacity of the daytime. Don't you?

POE
How did you know?

WOMAN
Only such a man would call after midnight. Although fascinating, the night is chilling; you would love a cup of hot coffee thick with brown sugar. You prefer brandy, for the chill, and hope I will offer, but would not be so rude as to request it from a lady.

POE
You are wrong about the brandy.

WOMAN
You want none?

POE
I am rude enough to ask for it.

WOMAN
You are forward, you know.

POE
I shouldn't think to take advantage of you.

> He turns to go. She reaches to stop him.

WOMAN
What are you doing here?

POE
I am calling in response to an advertisement in the Journal. The clothing.

WOMAN
The size forties?

POE
Of course.

WOMAN
Ah, yes. I sold them!

POE
All?

WHITMAN
Every piece.

POE
Your price was ridiculous!

WHITMAN
I lowered it for charity.

POE
How low?

WHITMAN
I gave them to the church for nothing.

POE
My waistcoat? My scarf, Sarah? I make little money as an
assistant, damnit, that scarf was the only piece of silk I
owned.

WHITMAN
I am sorry, Edgar. (falls sobbing onto bed) You shouldn't
have come!

POE
(jumps on her) You shouldn't have moved.

WHITMAN
It can't work, you know.

POE
That is your Ladies Club talking; jealous bitches every one.

WHITMAN
(snapping out of it) And to them you are the perfect adulterous bastard.

POE
Contempt spurred on, no doubt, by Mrs. Eliot!

WHITMAN
Of course.

POE
That damned zealot! The meddling hypocrite!

WHITMAN
She hates you.

POE
She hates me? Every moment you and I are together, she wishes to be in your place!

WHITMAN
Don't be disgusting, Edgar.

POE
Forgive me. I would debate her on the matter, with you our judge, but she lacks the brains to hold up her end; I have read letters written by her... the battle would prove most boring.

WHITMAN
Where would you read her letters?

POE
Uh, to the fashion editor. Something about the danger of ladies slit-sleeves promoting sexual activity. Why is it those who don't participate are so very concerned with those who do?

WHITMAN
(fingering her corset laces) Abstinence breeds obsession.

POE
I don't believe the abstaining is voluntary in her case.

WHITMAN
There's no one to tempt her.

POE
And, therefore, she is frustrated by everybody.

WHITMAN
Yes. (they kiss) Damn you, Poe.

POE
And you, Mrs. Whitman. (they kiss again.)

WHITMAN
Edgar, your hand is bleeding.

POE
I broke a bottle.

WHITMAN
I hope it was a full one. The cut is deep. (kisses his hand) What are we doing?

POE
May I stay tonight?

WHITMAN
Edgar, I've only moved here; what will my new neighbors say?

POE
You never paid heed to the gossip of your former neighbors.

WHITMAN
I told you I did not wish to see you again.

POE
I will oblige you, I promise. But please let me stay tonight. I can sleep on the chair.

WHITMAN
What's the matter?

POE
I can't be alone.

WHITMAN
Oh, Edgar.

POE
I'm afraid.

WHITMAN
(joking) What, spectres hovering about your head?

POE
More than you realize.

WHITMAN
Interesting for a man, who chooses the subjects you write, to fear the dark. Although, in the years since James died, my love for the night has grown stronger... therefore my fear has grown stronger, too.

POE
Do you think of him often?

WHITMAN
You have lost a love... do the passing years lessen the pain?

POE
No.

WHITMAN
Virginia would be happy to hear you say that.

POE
(Elmira) I wasn't thinking of Virginia.

WHITMAN
Edgar, you flatter me.

POE
(pause, a lie) Uh, yes.

WHITMAN
I guess there is no harm in a widower and a widow finding refuge from tormenting memories in each other's company.

POE
Thank you, Sarah.

WHITMAN
I'll fetch a bandage for your hand. (a warning) And
blankets for the chair.

> Poe sits. Whitman covers
> him with a blanket.

POE
Any brandy?

WHITMAN
No. (she kisses his forehead and climbs into bed)
Goodnight, Edgar.

> Poe finds paper, ink, and
> writes...

POE
"When reason returned with the morning -- when I had
slept off the fumes of the night's debauch -- " (crumples
paper)

> Whitman disturbed by the
> noise.

POE
(writing) "I experienced a sentiment half of horror, half of
remorse, for the crime of which I had been guilty." Oh...!
(crumples)

WHITMAN
Edgar, please.

POE
Of course. (writing) "But it was, at best, a feeble and
equivocal feeling and the soul remained..." -- damn!

> Whitman, witness to his writer's block, giggles from her bed.

POE
What?

WHITMAN
(laughing) Your silhouette looks like a chubby ghost.

POE
If only my demons were as amiable.

WHITMAN
(pause) Come to bed.

> Poe sits on the bed, kissing, undressing.
>
> Elmira enters interrupting foreplay.

POE
(resigned) Oh, no.

WHITMAN
What's the matter?

POE
I can't.

WHITMAN
Nonsense. (kisses him again, he steps away) Don't you love me? Edgar?

POE
(to Elmira) Now see what you've done.

ELMIRA
What have you done?

> A wave of Elmira's hand and
> Virginia has replaced
> Whitman in the bed. Poe is
> hunched over a desk, writing.

VIRGINIA
How is it?

POE
What?! Virginia? Oh, fine.

VIRGINIA
It's one in the morning, Eddy.

POE
Yes.

VIRGINIA
You'll be up all night.

POE
I'm writing. I need to write.

VIRGINIA
It's very cold, Eddy, aren't you coming to bed?

POE
No.

VIRGINIA
But you must. It's been two weeks since our wedding.

POE
Please, Virginia.

VIRGINIA
(reading over his shoulder) "The Black Cat. But it was, at best, a feeble and equivocal feeling, and the soul remained untouched."

POE
It's about a man who murders his wife.

VIRGINIA
Cheery. (grabs his pen) Ha, ha, I have it now!

POE
Virginia, give me the pen. Virginia.

VIRGINIA
(playing, hides it in her nightgown) Come and get it.

POE
Give it to me.

VIRGINIA
(sing song) "Try and find it!"

POE
(pounds the bed angrily, stops just short of slapping her) Give me the pen!

VIRGINIA
(she can't believe it) Eddy. Eddy?

POE
I'm sorry, Sissy. I'm sorry.

> Virginia lets her hair down, removes her nightgown.

POE
Virginia --

> She takes his head in her hands.

VIRGINIA
Love me, Eddy.

> Light change. Virginia is gone. Poe finds himself again on Whitman's bed.

ELMIRA
How long will you be unhappy?

POE
What do you want of me? Leave me alone! Leave me alone.

> The Specter exits.

WHITMAN
Edgar? Edgar. Wake up, you're having a nightmare. Are you all right?

POE
Yes. Yes.

WHITMAN
You were dreaming of Virginia. You called her name.

POE
You are so good to me. Why?

WHITMAN
(pause) The Raven, I think. Anyone who may feel such
pain may feel love as deeply. And I love you. Since James
passed away, I've known no other man. We are equals.
Poets. We are perfect for each other. I have never asked
you before, but have I been your only lover since Virginia?
(pause) Edgar? (fighting to stay calm) I guess that's really
too much to ask. I suppose the Ladies Club was right, and I
was right to move to the outskirts of the town --

POE
-- Sarah --

WHITMAN
-- get out, Edgar.

POE
But I need you, Sarah.

WHITMAN
Need me? Tell me you love me, and don't lie. (he can't)
Get out! Get out! I can't believe I let you in at all! Go! (she
forces him out) I've been deluding myself, I believed you
cared, but you don't... how many others do you have? Who
is this "Elmira?"

POE
Elmira?

WHITMAN
Your dream... you shouted her name, too!

Whitman exits.

POE
I knew her over twenty years ago! But she haunts me still. (after Whitman) There is no one else. There is no one at all. What about The Raven?

ELMIRA
(entering) What about The Raven?

POE
No, no, no. How do you follow me?

ELMIRA
A "tempest tossed me here from the night's Plutonic shore."

POE
Oh, shut up.

ELMIRA
Do you remember The Raven, Edgar?

> Virginia enters, bedridden, coughing.

POE
It took me months.

ELMIRA
Virginia contracted consumption.

POE
I worked day and night.

ELMIRA
Virginia grew worse.

POE
I was creating the most perfect poem!

ELMIRA
She gave you the blanket.

> Virginia covers Poe at desk.

POE
It was going to be my masterpiece. I spent our last pennies on paper and ink.

ELMIRA
Instead of firewood. She slept with a cat on her chest for the warmth. The cat seemed to know her function, performed it willingly.

POE
Once I sold the verse it would bring enough for a new home, new clothes.

ELMIRA
Perhaps, a doctor?

POE
It would bring me fame. "Ah, distinctly I remember, it was in the bleak December."

ELMIRA
An icy Winter... the worst time for poor Virginia.

POE
The Raven was a success!

ELMIRA
The consumption took hold.

Poe carries unconscious
Virginia in his arms.

POE
I conquered Europe! I conquered the United States!

ELMIRA
She would never be the same.

POE
At long last, I conquered you!

ELMIRA
Can you conquer yourself, Edgar?

POE
You would not love me... the people did.

ELMIRA
And, in return, you loved the people. Especially the
women. Poetry served you well, Edgar.

POE
I found sanctuary from torment in the writing. It soothed
my misery like a balm.

ELMIRA
The verses themselves became the very coals of fiery
anguish and confusion.

POE
What?

ELMIRA
Your love poetry, Edgar, has broken many hearts.

POE
No.

ELMIRA
Did you write to particular ladies, or were the verses
intended for the eyes of the world?

POE
The inspiration may have come from a few women...

> Poe sets Virginia on her feet.
> She recites Eulalie. (See
> appendix.)

VIRGINIA
I dwelt alone, in a world of moan, And my soul was a
stagnant tide Till the fair and gentle Eulalie became my
blushing bride -- (etc.)

> Unaware of each other, three
> more Women enter one after
> another until they are reciting
> simultaneously. Female
> Furies. Poe tormented.

> Mrs. Eliot reads For Annie.

MRS. ELIOT
...And so it lies happily, Bathing in many A dream of the
love And the beauty of Annie -- (etc.)

> Whitman reads To Helen.

WHITMAN
...All--all expired save thee--save less than thou: Save only
the divine light in thine eyes--Save but the soul in thine
uplifted eyes. (etc.)

> Mary reads Divine Right Of
> Kings.

MARY
...Her bosom is an ivory throne, Where tyrant virtue reigns alone; No subject vice dare interfere, To check the power that governs here. O! would she deign to rule my fate --

POE
No. No... Stop it. Stop it! Enough!

ELMIRA
The ink was wet from the first as you began the second, third, and fourth! All written in a single week to different women, each verse proclaiming your undying affection. Make no denial, Edgar.

MARY
He loves me.

MRS. ELIOT
He loves me.

WHITMAN
I forgive him.

VIRGINIA
I love you.

> Virginia kisses him and again
> collapses dead in his arms.

POE
The attention... after so long... I was overwhelmed. (crying) Oh, Virginia... what have I done? What have I done?

> Poe exits carrying Virginia's
> body.
>
> Lights down.
> The sound of a dry wind.
>
> Lights up.
> Newspaper office. Griswold
> alone composing a poem.

GRISWOLD
...Love... Dove... Mauve... uh, no.

> Mrs. Eliot and Blatherskite
> society friends enter.

GRISWOLD
(taken with women) Good day, Ladies. I am the Rev -- I
am Rufus Griswold, contributor.

> Poe enters.

GRISWOLD
And this is --

BLATHERSKITE #1
Edgar Poe, of course.

GRISWOLD
You've a following, Edgar, I told you so. Downright
famous.

BLATHERSKITE #2
Infamous.

POE
And infamy ain't pretty, Rufus. (annoyed) Mrs. Eliot, my
dear friend --

GRISWOLD
May we offer you some -- ?

MRS. ELIOT
-- That won't be necessary, Reverend. We are here on
business, personal business, but business all the same.

POE
Well, we are rushed to finish this page. You should leave
and return during reception hours, when there will be
someone of your mentality here to help you. Perhaps a
printer still dizzy and dimwitted from ink vapors.

MRS. ELIOT
You may hurl your insults, Mr. Poe. They bounce off us as
Goliath's spears bent on David's heavenly armor --

POE
I should have known you'd recruit God to your side.

MRS. ELIOT
-- mere sticks and stones -- like frail slings and arrows --

POE
-- Conjure Shakespeare to your argument and I will kill you.

GRISWOLD
Poe?!

POE
Why is it this slasher hasn't chosen targets whose
destruction would benefit society? Veritable vermin... and
fat sitting ducks at that!

MRS. ELIOT
Enough, Mr. Poe! I think you know why we are here.

POE
Actually, Mrs. Eliot, I have no idea. Unless it is to reaffirm your position as this town's ultracrepidarian.

BLATHERSKITE #1
(pause, then to Eliot) A "busybody." I think.

MRS. ELIOT
We are on a mission!

POE
Neither an angel or a devil would be without one.

MRS. ELIOT
Sarah Whitman has engaged us, myself and the Blatherskite sisters, to come to you and request --

BLATHERSKITE #2
-- demand --

BLATHERSKITE #1
--yes, demand --

MRS. ELIOT
-- demand the immediate return of certain letters she has written you over the past months while under the intoxicating influence of your love-lies and the like. I, we, realize said letters are probably at your home, but felt it would be improper to make inquiry there, so we have come to your place of employ --

POE
(pulls stack of letters from desk) Take them, burn them,
anything, but please shut up.

MRS. ELIOT
They were here. You keep them here so that no one of your
many other lovers would find them and know the truth!

POE
I hadn't thought of that, Mrs. Eliot.

MRS. ELIOT
Her love-letters! Her poetry! Concealed here from other
duped women who would find themselves lying awake and
restless between your sheets while you snored alongside
post-fornication.

POE
-- Splendid use of imagery --

MRS. ELIOT
(too vehement) Do you know what these are? Do you?
This is the precious outpouring of that woman's heart. The
heart you misled, the heart you tore with your folly, your
inauspicious meanderings, your infidelity! (crossing
herself) Oh, God forgive you, Poe. There is nothing left in
your adulterous soul. Come along, ladies. (turns to exit)

POE
Miss Blatherskite? (hands them a second stack) While you
are on mercy errands, perhaps you would deliver these to
one of the other duped women who found herself lying
awake between my sheets?

MRS. ELIOT
What are those?

POE
Love-letters from another innocent sinner whose only
desire was to soil my bedclothes, had she not torn them
away altogether, all grabbing hands and teeth -- (shudders)

MRS. ELIOT
Give them to me. Give them to me!

> They read. Then, look
> daggers at uncovered Mrs.
> Eliot.

BLATHERSKITES
Mrs. Eliot, for shame!

> They exit.

MRS. ELIOT
Oh, Edgar. You loathsome disgusting degenerate!

> Mrs. Eliot exits.

POE
Good day, Mrs. Eliot.

GRISWOLD
Ahhh, Poe... what have you done?

> Mrs. Eliot re-enters with a
> stuffed Raven and shoves it in
> Griswold's hands.

MRS. ELIOT
Here, Reverend, give this to that man. I no longer care to
have it above my bedchamber door.

Mrs. Eliot exits.

POE
How perfectly gaudy.

GRISWOLD
Yes. But you really must change your ways, Edgar. Loving so many, uh, "dilutes" your affections. And makes for numerous enemies, the least of which is not yourself.

POE
Guiding words from the pastor?

GRISWOLD
Words of observation from a friend. Your straying will come back and haunt you.

POE
Amen.

The Inspector enters.

POE
You're in time for this issue, Inspector. Any gristlies you'd care to add? Is the fiend still doing his bit to further American literature?

GRISWOLD
Poe.

POE
Forgive my anxiousness; I am eager to read the work of so ruthless a plagiarist.

INSPECTOR
This time it was another's work.

GRISWOLD
There was a killing? (Inspector hands Griswold a report)
Oh, God.

INSPECTOR
With a development; it seems the victim got off a shot from
her pistol. We can't tell if her assailant was hit, there was
so much blood everywhere from the lady, but we're on the
lookout at all hospitals for a ball wound.

GRISWOLD
Did he leave a message?

INSPECTOR
Oh, yes. The department assures me the sentences were
not of Mr. Poe's work. They've checked every published
volume... took fifteen men.

POE
I had no idea I was so prolific.

INSPECTOR
Though the lines are as miserable, the work is not yours.

POE
Our boy is growing wise. Probably picked a passage from
Oliver Twist so he can slash twenty more women while
you're off in London pestering poor old Dickens!

INSPECTOR
Or you are trying to throw me off your track, Mr. Poe.

POE
Impossible. You're too shrewd. Recite the passage.
Please.

INSPECTOR
That's private to the investigation.

POE
I might be of some help.

INSPECTOR
You were permitted to know the others because they were
yours... and Daniel prodded me on, so.

POE
Where is the Constable?

INSPECTOR
Ill.

POE
Send him my best, will you? He'll have your job someday.
He has a good mind... a shame to waste it in such an office.

INSPECTOR
I'll not be a target of your ridicule, Mr. Poe.

POE
Forgive me. You're correct, of course; it is better to waste
the efforts of fifteen men, pouring over volumes of
literature to find an elusive passage, rather than swallow
your pride and make inquiry of one well-versed in the field
who could probably discover the origin of the written clue
immediately.

GRISWOLD
We are experts, Inspector.

INSPECTOR
Very well. (a page) This was found last night on the body of Mrs. Michelle Robins. (frightening Griswold) The note was pinned to her tongue... severed and lying some arm's length from her corpse.

GRISWOLD
(gulp) I don't recognize it. How about you, Poe?

POE
It is reminiscent of something German. (to Inspector) I'll check the library, if you wish.

INSPECTOR
I would appreciate that. Discovering the origin of the work might give me more insight on this lunatic. Well, I'm off. I must investigate some five or six hospitals... by the way, what happened to your hand, Mr. Poe?

POE
Nothing so dramatic as a gunshot wound, Inspector. I was bitten by an irate lady. I left her very much alive, I assure you.

INSPECTOR
May I look at it?

POE
No. You might have your men make a dental impression, match teeth all over the city, and discover the identity of the woman. I'd find myself and the lady amidst a scandal. My sense of honor prevents it.

INSPECTOR
Good day, Reverend.

Inspector exits.

GRISWOLD
He's really a very good fellow, you know.

POE
(eyeing the note) What? Oh, yes. You're certain you don't recognize this?

GRISWOLD
Quite.

POE
Rufus... I'm going out. To the library. Can you manage the page without me?

GRISWOLD
Mr. Briggs wants it this afternoon.

POE
(adamant) Will you manage without me?

GRISWOLD
If I must. Yes.

Poe exits.

Griswold sets the note aside and works on the newspaper.

Briggs enters, hurrying.

BRIGGS
There was another murder, Rufus.

GRISWOLD
We know.

BRIGGS
The other dailies have joined the hunt. All carry bloody news of the slasher. As nauseating as it sounds, we must keep in step. We need details about the murders.

GRISWOLD
The Inspector was just here.

BRIGGS
Good! Did you interview him?

GRISWOLD
Poe and myself.

BRIGGS
Were there any developments?

GRISWOLD
(preoccupied with his work) Only this. A quote found on the body. As he has aptly demonstrated, this slasher has it in for the fairer sex. The Inspector has enlisted Poe to help; he's gone to the library to discover the source of the passage.

BRIGGS
(reads note) Well, he won't find it there.

GRISWOLD
What do you mean?

BRIGGS
It hasn't been published, yet.

GRISWOLD
It's familiar to you?

BRIGGS
I am the editor. (reads) "The thousand injuries of woman I had borne as best I could; but when they ventured upon insult, I vowed revenge."

GRISWOLD
Yes. Where have you seen it?

BRIGGS
This is a paraphrasing of the opening sentence of Poe's newest story.

GRISWOLD
(shocked) What?

> They exit.
>
> Danny's House.
> Danny seated, reading. He has a full bookshelf and a tall cabinet.
>
> On a table beside him rests a jar with something floating inside.
>
> A knock.
>
> He favors his arm as he answers. Edgar Poe is on the other side.

POE
Hello, Daniel.

DANNY
I've been expecting you, Edgar. Let me take your coat.

> Poe removes his coat
> revealing a pistol.

DANNY
That won't be necessary.

POE
I feel better carrying it. How is your arm?

DANNY
I have been wounded before by... them. Mrs. Robins was a poor shot.

POE
To her great disappointment.

DANNY
(laughs) Yes. May I get you a drink? Something to eat, perhaps?

POE
What, kidney?

DANNY
(laughs) Oh, we are alike.

POE
No.

DANNY
Are you certain?

POE
You are a monster.

DANNY
Yes. Oh, yes. You have conjured me. And I will do your bidding because you cannot.

POE
My bidding?

DANNY
I see everything. In your stories.

POE
You've implicated me, Daniel.

DANNY
I could never harm you, Edgar.

POE
Only you, myself, and Briggs have laid eyes on that passage; when published it would have steered Mulhearn straight to me.

DANNY
Such evidence isn't enough to arrest you. I have kept you safe. I didn't leave your words to have you fall for the task I perform, no, Edgar. I left them in honor of you. Amontillado was my method of letting you know it was me. I could never harm you. In fact, I have destroyed one whose intention was to do you an injustice.

POE
Mary.

> Saloon music.
> Lights up on Mary.

DANNY
I saw her. At the saloon. The men were leering at her.
Lascivious wolves. And she teased them, she teased them
all. She let them think they could have her and she danced
and she sang and she touched them... their hair their faces
their mouths. I felt pity for them... for all the wolves at the
bar... and then I realized I, also, was seated on a stool, I
held a mug of beer, I was one of the line of wolves and the
pity I was feeling was for myself! I hated it. I hated her. I
cannot stand being pitied for I am not pitiful. I stood to
leave. I had my coat in my hand and was all but out the
door when -- when she said something horrible --

POE
-- what Daniel? What? Did she chide a drunkard for
fondling her? Did she take money?

DANNY
She mentioned you. Bragging how the famous Edgar Allan
Poe had been in love with her! (this halts Poe)

MARY
Years ago, when he was first starting. The poor thing, he
vowed we could never be merely friends, which is what I
desired, because he was so enraptured with me. It's true.
Why, in that poem, The Raven, he mentions me, I am the
woman he lost; the "fair and radiant maiden" --

DANNY
-- "rare... and radiant maiden."

MARY
Why, yes.

DANNY
(walking) You knew him.

MARY
Not as much as he would have had it.

DANNY
And he said those things?

MARY
More. He was eloquent. He said it would only pain him to be platonic.

DANNY
Of course. But not because he loved you.

MARY
He said he could not stand being my friend.

DANNY
Why would Edgar Poe want to be friends with a willing harlot who has no brains at all?

MARY
What's that?

DANNY
Why should he spend time with a body that is good for only one base function, and not be allowed to partake of that function?

MARY
Oh, come on, you're spoiling my mood --

DANNY
(a hand over her mouth) Yes.

Lights out on Mary.

Lights up on Poe and Danny.

DANNY
You confirmed all when you described her to the Inspector.
She lived to be the object of men's adoration. I molded her
in accord with her wishes and she has become a trophy.

POE
She was beautiful.

DANNY
Pretty pretty Mary. That is the reason I killed her, Edgar.
That is our reason. I couldn't stand to hear her, and her
poor excuse for a mind, talk about you like that. I did it for
you. She was my first.

POE
You mean to continue.

DANNY
I mean to do the work that you in your position cannot do.
I know how you feel about them. I see it in your stories.

POE
What do you see, Daniel?

DANNY
Your feelings about women. The pain they have caused
you.

POE
You are gravely mistaken, Daniel.

DANNY
The women in your work are vermin to be erased.

POE
Oh, an art lesson?

DANNY
An artist creates the world he would live in.

POE
Yes.

DANNY
So do I.

POE
Your world is a hideous one.

DANNY
(laughs) You're one to talk! How do you feel about women, Edgar? You've destroyed many.

POE
(a weak defense) Stories.

DANNY
Murder victims.

POE
My heroines die of causes considered natural. I mourn them.

DANNY
You do not kill them?

POE
No.

DANNY
Not Berenice?

POE
Epilepsy.

DANNY
Eleonora?

POE
Consumption.

DANNY
The Lady Usher?

POE
Catalepsy.

DANNY
Morella?

POE
Dead in childbirth.

DANNY
The Black Cat? -- I suggest a wife who succumbs to an ax in the brain is a victim --

POE
-- Acknowledged.

DANNY
Lenore?

POE
Consumption.

DANNY
Annabel Lee?

POE
Consumption.

DANNY
Rowena?

POE
(pause) Pneumonia --

DANNY
-- she died of an unnamed illness --

POE
-- I'm naming it now!

DANNY
(a smile) Very well... The Wife of the Oval Portrait?

POE
(weakening) Neglect.

DANNY
Ulalume.

POE
Consumption.

DANNY
Irene.

POE
Consumption.

DANNY
Ligeia?

POE
(fighting tears) Consumption.

DANNY
(pause) Shall I go on?

POE
(shaking his head) Diseases. From the hand of God.

DANNY
Murder victims. Cut off with a stroke of your pen.

POE
(weakened, sitting) I do mourn them.

DANNY
(The gun doesn't frighten him. He pours Poe one. Poe drinks.) It's all right... I feel the same way. And as you wield a pen for me -- as you tell the world how horrible their crimes are -- I wield a dagger for you, for us, to help put an end to those crimes.

POE
Crimes?

DANNY
Of all men, I know you understand best.

POE
What? What?

DANNY
Jezebel. Woman. While we work to further ourselves, they develop beauty instead of hearts. Like useless jewels ever out of reach of the common man. They lie. They shun learning. They are false friends. (lightly) You know, they grow angry with you when you give them good advice? They'll enlist your mind for guidance in some problem, listen attentively to your suggestions for change, agree with those ideas, then continue on in their sing-song self-destructive behavior, without me, knowing their pretty faces will see them through in the end. Their faces. Ah, yes, how I have fixed their faces!

POE
(aims pistol) You can't know what I feel.

DANNY
I do, Edgar, because I, too, have fallen for a painted face and wished to see it decay before me. Because I have hated for loving. Because I have denied my principles for the touch of a woman only to have her cackle in my face in a dark bedroom. You are afraid of the dark?

POE
Everyone has spectres who take shape once the lamps are dim -- I am terrified, still, by such things.

DANNY
I was, too. But now, the macabre has become the everyday. We embrace the terrible. Read the papers. Hear the gossip. See the fear on the faces of the shop girls who must pass through this neighborhood. Notice the gate of those who travel wide round to avoid altogether the "monster who tears women." After much work -- and wonderful publicity -- like a nightmare, I am the thing people fear in the dark.

POE
A nightmare is halted with the morning light.

DANNY
You find relief in your work by reproducing that which you despise -- you control them in your stories just as savages construct an enemy's likeness in miniature. You should be commended, Edgar, for your art. That's why I love you. Myself, I need no voodoo dolls; the women, our enemies, fall blind and unarmed into my trap, as you and I once fell innocently into the snare of their dangerous beauty.

> Danny gently takes the gun
> and opens the door for
> stunned Poe.

DANNY
You are an author, your work furthers our cause; go and write. I am an exterminator... leave me to my business.

POE
Daniel? What about women who do not endeavor to make their way through the grace of their good looks? What about those industrious ones who work for a purpose? What about women who are plain?

DANNY
Have you ever met one who would not willingly trade a bit of her character to become a bit more beautiful?

> Poe exits.

> Danny takes the jar from the
> table and tosses it and
> catches it again.

DANNY
Pretty pretty Mary.

> He opens the cabinet doors revealing a hundred like jars... each containing a souvenir.
>
> Lights down on Danny.
>
> Lights up on Poe walking on street.
>
> Whitman sees Poe and turns snobbishly the other way.
>
> Poe is deep in thought and does not notice her.

WHITMAN
I appreciate the effort, Edgar.

POE
What?

WHITMAN
At ignoring me.

POE
Oh.

WHITMAN
I know it was an act; you've never been so wrapped in thought that you didn't notice my perfume. You look as though you've seen a ghost.

POE
Nothing so ordinary.

WHITMAN
It's good to see you.

POE
Yes, well, I really must be going.

WHITMAN
For a whiskey, no doubt.

POE
Absolutely.

WHITMAN
I'll not accept the blame... for breaking your heart and driving you to drink.

POE
(laughs) Rest assured. (turns to go)

WHITMAN
(stopping him) I understand you gave Mrs. Eliot the going over. She probably deserved it.

POE
If I remember, yes.

WHITMAN
(pause, something in her wants him still) How are you, my Raven?

POE
I have seen my murky reflection and my life is horribly clear to me now.

WHITMAN
I owe you an apology, Edgar. For expecting too much, and blaming you when you did not live up to those expectations. I knew you wrote The Raven to mend your own broken heart. I thought you composed it and transcended your condition. I was mistaken. You shall truly be lifted nevermore, and your life since has been a lie. I was guilty of hoping otherwise. Your work. Your time with me. Your time with Virginia. All for nothing while you waited for your hopeless heart to beat its feeble lonely last.

POE
Alliteration. Very good.

WHITMAN
Do you agree with my theory, Edgar?

POE
Um, yes?

WHITMAN
-- No!

POE
-- No --

WHITMAN
-- There's no such thing as a hopelessly broken heart!

POE
Oh, I would spare you the clarity... you who would peer into my maelstrom.

WHITMAN
Edgar. Perhaps, someday, we may start again.

POE
I don't deserve you.

WHITMAN
When will I see you, Edgar?

POE
Whoa, what?

WHITMAN
When will I see you again?

POE
(giggling) Quoth the Raven... etcetera.

> With no regards for
> Whitman, Poe laughs loudly
> and turns to go.
>
> Whitman grabs his lapel.

WHITMAN
Edgar!

> Poe grabs her throat.

POE
Sarah! Do you know there is a madman loose? That he
would as willingly use your tendons for saddle laces as let
you breathe? On this day, today, anyone may commit a foul
carving murder, attach a note, and have the blame lie with
that madman? Mrs. Whitman, hold your tongue in check
and test me not with theories on hearts metaphorically
broken, or you may find yours torn and mangled in your
lap. Leave me alone. Please.

Poe exits.

Whitman wipes her tears
with a handkerchief.

WHITMAN
The bastard.

She composes herself,
manages to drop her
handkerchief, then exits the
direction opposite Poe.

Danny enters, smiles in the
direction of Poe, finds the
handkerchief, and exits after
Whitman.

DANNY
Excuse me, pretty lady...

Poe's house. He goes for a
bottle.

Elmira enters.

ELMIRA
What have you done?

POE
Go away!

ELMIRA
I will stay. In this time of abominable horror, when you should be gnawing your teeth out of your head, when you should be lamenting the atrocious depravity of that boy, but instead contemplate like crimes yourself, I will stay. I will show you what you are. When deeds as heinous as his and yours become the everyday, hope for you is all but lost, Edgar Allan Poe. And as you fall into your pit, I would have you glimpse the path that brought you to it! On this day of misery, I remind you of a day of celebration. That which would have permitted you to be forever happy shall be that which makes you forever contemptible.

> Lights up.
> Brigg's parlor.

ELMIRA
Years ago. Valentine's Day. A gathering. And the guest of honor...

> Eliot, Virginia, Griswold,
> Briggs, listen to Whitman
> recite to Poe.

WHITMAN
"Oh! thou grim and ancient Raven, From the Night's plutonic shore..." (continues in mute)

ELMIRA
Learned lines.

POE
To express respect for her tutor.

WHITMAN
(finishing) "Not a bird that roams the forest, Shall our lofty eyrie share."

ELMIRA
(to Poe) Respect? To propose the erection of a lovenest?

GUESTS
Beautiful. Splendid... (Whitman sits) Good work, dear.

> Virginia watches as Whitman
> takes Poe's hand and looks
> into his eyes a little too long.

BRIGGS
Virginia?

VIRGINIA
It's not so good as Mrs. Whitman's or Mrs. Eliot's. I have
little schooling --

BRIGGS
Nonsense, my dear, take center stage.

> Virginia stands weakly, puts a
> hand to her chest. Coughs.

BRIGGS
Would you rather sit?

VIRGINIA
I'll be all right. "A Valentine." (clears congested throat,
then proceeds with all the love in the world.)

Ever with thee I wish to roam –
Dearest my life is thine.
Give me a cottage for my home
And a rich old cypress vine...

Removed from the world with its sin and care

(for Whitman and Eliot) And the tattling of many tongues.
Love alone shall guide us when we are there --
Love shall heal my weakened lungs;...

And Oh, the tranquil hours we'll spend,
Never wishing that others may see!
Perfect ease we'll enjoy, without thinking to lend
Ourselves to the world and its glee --
Ever peaceful and blissful we'll be.

MRS. ELIOT
(Exiting) The metre is poor.

GRISWOLD
(Exiting with Briggs) The rhyme is forced.

WHITMAN
It's juvenile.

VIRGINIA
The first letters of each line... they spell your name, darling.

ELMIRA
It's perfect.

POE
Brimming with love. Virginia, poor Virginia.

Virginia climbs in bed, alone.

VIRGINIA
Eddy... I dream of you.

ELMIRA
That night you made love...

> Whitman kisses Poe.

ELMIRA
...to your Sarah Helen Whitman. Were you home instead, beside your wife, perhaps you could have saved her from choking on her own breath.

> Poe goes to Virginia's bedside, holds her body.

POE
Virginia? Virginia? (to Elmira) I couldn't love her because of the haunting memories of you --

ELMIRA
Tears that never dry make you blind. Virginia was the best thing that ever happened to you, Elmira or no Elmira.

POE
-- I sent a hundred letters. I loved you and you didn't know it!

ELMIRA
Your resentment has become hatred and your hatred has blossomed into misery when, with Virginia, it could have been happiness.

POE
-- Virginia --

ELMIRA
Your loving bride was as dedicated to you as you were bound to your painful past.

POE
Virginia! Please! (rubbing her hands, striving to bring life back into her)

ELMIRA
She died in your bed while you sweated in Whitman's.

POE
Stop it.

ELMIRA
Your disillusionment has spoiled all hope for love in this life --

POE
Stop. Stop.

ELMIRA
-- your poor pathetic spirit shall be lifted nevermore --

POE
Please --

ELMIRA
-- seeks refuge instead in the beds of many women --

POE
I hate you.

ELMIRA
-- and has planted within you the seeds that have become a jungle and provided sanctuary for a murderer --

POE
Enough!

ELMIRA
-- as if gentle Virginia's death was not adequate payment for Elmira's so-called "crime!"

POE
Damn you to hell!

ELMIRA
-- I am you, Edgar --

POE
-- No!

> Poe hurls a bottle at Elmira's specter shattering the mirror.
>
> The memory of Virginia is gone from the bed.
>
> Poe is alone.

POE
Virginia? Elmira?

> Poe finds a large fragment of mirror and gazes at his reflection.

POE
What says my grim conscience, oh, spectre in my path?

> He presses the glass to his throat, pauses, stashes it in his pocket, and exits quickly.

> Lights up on Danny's house.
>
> Danny places an opium vial among his jars.
>
> Poe enters.

DANNY
I thought you'd come back. After talking that way to her.

POE
Who?

DANNY
You gave her an awful fright. But that's what we're good at, isn't it?

POE
It has been my curse.

DANNY
Your work is a gift. But now you are ready to partake of non-fiction.

POE
What do you mean?

DANNY
You're here to destroy that which you hate.

POE
Oh, yes.

DANNY
I'll show you. We'll have plenty of time with no possibility of discovery. It's your first... I reckoned even you would be nervous.

> Danny reveals unconscious Whitman.

POE
Sarah.

DANNY
I gave her laudanum. You want the honors?

POE
Very much.

> Danny turns his back to select a knife and jars. Poe inches closer to him.

DANNY
Where you gonna do it? Heart? Throat?

POE
You should have taken up the rodeo, Daniel.

DANNY
What's that?

POE
Heart, I think.

> The Constable turns. Poe plunges the glass into Danny's torso.

DANNY
What have you done? What have you d -- ? (falls)

POE
Sarah! Sarah! Wake up. Come on. (lifts her to her feet)
That's it. That's it, my Helen.

> Danny interlocks his fingers,
> hits the Poet hard on the back
> of the neck, then falls dead.
>
> Poe staggers downstage
> without Whitman.
>
> The Inspector, Briggs,
> Griswold unaware of Poe.

GRISWOLD
Oh, Mrs. Whitman! Are you all right?

INSPECTOR
-- she stabbed him in the struggle –

> Chaos. Confusion.

POE
He got me a good one.

> Deputy Clell enters near Poe.

DEPUTY
Drinking again, eh, Mr. Poe?

INSPECTOR
-- We could use with a bit of help in here, Deputy!

Deputy hurries to crime scene.

Lights down on crime scene.

POE
Oh, he got me good indeed.

Virginia's Spectre enters, takes Poe's hands... Death.

VIRGINIA
Dance with me, Eddy.

Poe kisses her. Then, a bittersweet waltz.

They exit.

Lights up on Graveyard.

Briggs, Griswold, Whitman, Eliot, Inspector, and Ladies present at Poe's funeral.

The real Elmira stands beside husband Shelton.

Griswold steps aside to write the obituary.

GRISWOLD
-- after four days in the hospital, never fully regaining consciousness, Edgar Allan Poe died peacefully of what appeared to be exhaustion resulting from alcohol shock. His funeral was attended by some friends and professional acquaintances... women propagating.

> The funeral ends. The friends go separate ways.

SHELTON
I'll bring the carriage, Elmira. (the name halts Whitman)

> Shelton exits.

WHITMAN
Elmira?

ELMIRA ROYSTER SHELTON
Yes?

WHITMAN
How did you know him?

ELMIRA ROYSTER SHELTON
Edgar Poe and I went to public school together. We were children. I had a crush on him.

WHITMAN
Did he return your affections?

ELMIRA ROYSTER SHELTON
(pause) It was so long ago. I -- I don't remember.

THE CURTAIN FALLS

APPENDIX

These verses are recited and overlapped during the Female
Furies sequence:

EULALIE
(Read by Virginia)
    I dwelt alone
    In a world of moan,
And my soul was a stagnant tide
Till the fair and gentle Eulalie
became my blushing bride --
Till the yellow-haired young
Eulalie became my smiling bride.

    Ah, less, less bright
    The stars of the night
Than the eyes of the radiant girl,
    And never a flake
    That the vapor can make
With the morn-tints of purple
and pearl
Can vie with the modest Eulalie's
most unregarded curl --
Can compare with the bright-eyed
Eulalie's most humble and careless curl. (etc.)

      FOR ANNIE
       (Read by Mrs. Eliot)
    ...And so it lies happily,
    Bathing in many
    A dream of the love
    And the beauty of Annie --
    Drowned in a bath
    Of the tresses of Annie.

She tenderly kissed me,
She fondly caressed,
And then I fell gently
To sleep on her breast --
Deeply to sleep
From the heaven of her breast.

...my heart it is brighter
Than all of the many
Stars of heaven
For it sparkles with Annie --
It glows with the fire
Of the love of my Annie --
With the thought of the light
Of the eyes of my Annie. (etc.)

TO HELEN
 (Read by Whitman)
...All--all expired save thee--save less than thou:
Save only the divine light in thine eyes--
Save but the soul in thine uplifted eyes.
I saw but them--they were the world to me.
I saw but them--saw only them for hours--
Saw only them until the moon went down.
What wild heart-histories seemed to lie enwritten
Upon those crystalline, celestial spheres!
How dark a woe! yet how sublime a hope!
How silently serene a sea of pride!
How daring an ambition! yet how deep--
How fathomless a capacity for love! (etc.)

THE RAVEN

Once upon a midnight dreary, while I pondered weak and weary,
Over many a quaint and curious volume of forgotten lore,
While I nodded, nearly napping, suddenly there came a tapping,
As of some one gently rapping, rapping at my chamber door.
`'Tis some visitor,' I muttered, `tapping at my chamber door -
Only this, and nothing more.'

Ah, distinctly I remember it was in the bleak December,
And each separate dying ember wrought its ghost upon the floor.
Eagerly I wished the morrow; - vainly I had sought to borrow
From my books surcease of sorrow - sorrow for the lost Lenore -
For the rare and radiant maiden whom the angels named Lenore -
Nameless here for evermore.

And the silken sad uncertain rustling of each purple curtain
Thrilled me - filled me with fantastic terrors never felt before;
So that now, to still the beating of my heart, I stood repeating
`'Tis some visitor entreating entrance at my chamber door -
Some late visitor entreating entrance at my chamber door; -
This it is, and nothing more,'

Presently my soul grew stronger; hesitating then no longer,
`Sir,' said I, `or Madam, truly your forgiveness I implore;
But the fact is I was napping, and so gently you came rapping,
And so faintly you came tapping, tapping at my chamber door,
That I scarce was sure I heard you' - here I opened wide the door; -
Darkness there, and nothing more.

Deep into that darkness peering, long I stood there wondering, fearing,
Doubting, dreaming dreams no mortal ever dared to dream before
But the silence was unbroken, and the darkness gave no token,
And the only word there spoken was the whispered word, `Lenore!'
This I whispered, and an echo murmured back the word, `Lenore!'
Merely this and nothing more.

Back into the chamber turning, all my soul within me burning,
Soon again I heard a tapping somewhat louder than before.
`Surely,' said I, `surely that is something at my window lattice;
Let me see then, what thereat is, and this mystery explore -
Let my heart be still a moment and this mystery explore; -
'Tis the wind and nothing more!'

Open here I flung the shutter, when, with many a flirt and flutter,
In there stepped a stately raven of the saintly days of yore.
Not the least obeisance made he; not a minute stopped or stayed he;
But, with mien of lord or lady, perched above my chamber door -
Perched upon a bust of Pallas just above my chamber door -
Perched, and sat, and nothing more.

Then this ebony bird beguiling my sad fancy into smiling,
By the grave and stern decorum of the countenance it wore,
`Though thy crest be shorn and shaven, thou,' I said, `art sure no craven.
Ghastly grim and ancient raven wandering from the nightly shore -
Tell me what thy lordly name is on the Night's Plutonian shore!'
Quoth the raven, `Nevermore.'

Much I marvelled this ungainly fowl to hear discourse so plainly,
Though its answer little meaning - little relevancy bore;
For we cannot help agreeing that no living human being
Ever yet was blessed with seeing bird above his chamber door -
Bird or beast above the sculptured bust above his chamber door,
With such name as `Nevermore.'

But the raven, sitting lonely on the placid bust, spoke only,
That one word, as if his soul in that one word he did outpour.
Nothing further then he uttered - not a feather then he fluttered -
Till I scarcely more than muttered `Other friends have flown before -
On the morrow he will leave me, as my hopes have flown before.'
Then the bird said, `Nevermore.'

Startled at the stillness broken by reply so aptly spoken,
`Doubtless,' said I, `what it utters is its only stock and store,
Caught from some unhappy master whom unmerciful disaster
Followed fast and followed faster till his songs one burden bore -
Till the dirges of his hope that melancholy burden bore
Of "Never-nevermore."'

But the raven still beguiling all my sad soul into smiling,
Straight I wheeled a cushioned seat in front of bird and bust and door;
Then, upon the velvet sinking, I betook myself to linking
Fancy unto fancy, thinking what this ominous bird of yore -
What this grim, ungainly, ghastly, gaunt, and ominous bird of yore
Meant in croaking `Nevermore.'

This I sat engaged in guessing, but no syllable expressing
To the fowl whose fiery eyes now burned into my bosom's core;
This and more I sat divining, with my head at ease reclining
On the cushion's velvet lining that the lamp-light gloated o'er,
But whose velvet violet lining with the lamp-light gloating o'er,
She shall press, ah, nevermore!

Then, methought, the air grew denser, perfumed from an unseen censer
Swung by Seraphim whose foot-falls tinkled on the tufted floor.
`Wretch,' I cried, `thy God hath lent thee - by these angels he has sent thee
Respite - respite and nepenthe from thy memories of Lenore!
Quaff, oh quaff this kind nepenthe, and forget this lost Lenore!'
Quoth the raven, `Nevermore.'

`Prophet!' said I, `thing of evil! - prophet still, if bird or devil! -
Whether tempter sent, or whether tempest tossed thee here ashore,
Desolate yet all undaunted, on this desert land enchanted -
On this home by horror haunted - tell me truly, I implore -
Is there - is there balm in Gilead? - tell me - tell me, I implore!'
Quoth the raven, `Nevermore.'

`Prophet!' said I, `thing of evil! - prophet still, if bird or devil!
By that Heaven that bends above us - by that God we both adore -
Tell this soul with sorrow laden if, within the distant Aidenn,
It shall clasp a sainted maiden whom the angels named Lenore -
Clasp a rare and radiant maiden, whom the angels named Lenore?'
Quoth the raven, `Nevermore.'

`Be that word our sign of parting, bird or fiend!' I shrieked upstarting-
`Get thee back into the tempest and the Night's Plutonian shore!
Leave no black plume as a token of that lie thy soul hath spoken!
Leave my loneliness unbroken! - quit the bust above my door!
Take thy beak from out my heart, and take thy form from off my door!'
Quoth the raven, `Nevermore.'

And the raven, never flitting, still is sitting, still is sitting
On the pallid bust of Pallas just above my chamber door;
And his eyes have all the seeming of a demon's that is dreaming,
And the lamp-light o'er him streaming throws his shadow on the floor;
And my soul from out that shadow that lies floating on the floor
Shall be lifted - nevermore!

About the Author

Lawrence Riggins, MFA, screenwriter, playwright, director, story consultant, producer and member of the Writers Guild of America. He has written for SONY, The Ruddy-Morgan Organization, Millennium Films, Paramount Pictures, 21st Century, ABC Television, Atlantis, MGM, FOX, Showtime, Sci-Fi Channel, USA Network, and numerous Independent Feature Film and Television companies. He has won more than thirty film and theatre writing honors including the Samuel Goldwyn, Jack Nicholson, Chesterfield, Writers Digest, Laughing Horse, Cyclone, Thunderbird, Screenplay Festival, Script Shark, and Lawrence Thor awards.

<u>Awards for Seed of Darkness</u>
Morton R. Sarett Playwriting Competition Winner
Harrisburg Theatre New Play Festival Award Winner
Northern Kentucky University Y.E.S. New Play Festival Winner
Writers Digest Stage Play Competition Honorable Mention
Weissberger Playwriting Competition Semi-Finalist
West Coast Ensemble Full-Length Competition Runner-Up
Ferndale Rep New Works Competition Finalist
Wichita State University Nat'l Playwriting Contest Honorable Mention
Theatre Memphis New Play Competition Finalist
Writers Network Semi-Finalist

www.ingramcontent.com/pod-product-compliance
Lightning Source LLC
LaVergne TN
LVHW011235080426
835509LV00005B/503